UNDERSTANDING
BUDDHISM

BY A. W. BUCKEY

CONTENT CONSULTANT

Constance Kassor

Assistant Professor of Religious Studies
Lawrence University

Essential Library

An Imprint of Abdo Publishing | abdopublishing.com

UNDERSTANDING
WORLD RELIGIONS
AND BELIEFS

ABDOPUBLISHING.COM

Published by Abdo Publishing, a division of ABDO, PO Box 398166, Minneapolis, Minnesota 55439. Copyright © 2019 by Abdo Consulting Group, Inc. International copyrights reserved in all countries. No part of this book may be reproduced in any form without written permission from the publisher. Essential Library™ is a trademark and logo of Abdo Publishing.

Printed in the United States of America, North Mankato, Minnesota
042018
092018

Cover Photo: Vincent St. Thomas/Shutterstock Images
Interior Photos: Lim Yaohui/SPH Editorial Use Only/Newscom, 4–5; Jung Yeon Je/AFP/Getty Images, 7; AP Images, 8–9; Creative Touch Imaging Ltd/ZumaPress/Newscom, 10–11; Karleen Stevens/iStockphoto, 14–15; Wellcome Images/Science Source, 20–21; Ann Ronan Pictures/Heritage Images/Glow Images, 24; Neo Photo/iStockphoto, 26–27; Amos Chapple/REX/Shutterstock, 29; iStockphoto, 32–33, 38–39, 67, 80–81, 94–95; Santi Photo SS/Shutterstock Images, 36–37; Kathy Willens/AP Images, 43; Saikat Paul/Pacific Press/Sipa USA/AP Images, 49; Vietnam Stock Images/Shutterstock Images, 50–51; Vichan Poti/ZUMA Press/Newscom, 54–55; Shutterstock Images, 59, 61, 98–99; Stuart Jenner/Shutterstock Images, 62–63; Philippe Lissac/Godong/picture alliance/Godong/Newscom, 68; New York Public Library/Science Source, 70–71; Shane Myers Photography/Shutterstock Images, 76–77; Mark Maynard/The Herald Bulletin/AP Images, 79; Sk Hasan Ali/Shutterstock Images, 83; Chiang Ying-ying/AP Images, 85; Design Facts/Shutterstock Images, 90–91

Editor: Marie Pearson
Series Designer: Maggie Villaume

LIBRARY OF CONGRESS CONTROL NUMBER: 2017961378

PUBLISHER'S CATALOGING-IN-PUBLICATION DATA

Name: Buckey, A. W., author.
Title: Understanding Buddhism / by A. W. Buckey.
Description: Minneapolis, Minnesota : Abdo Publishing, 2019. | Series: Understanding world religions and beliefs | Includes online resources and index.
Identifiers: ISBN 9781532114236 (lib.bdg.) | ISBN 9781532154065 (ebook)
Subjects: LCSH: Buddhism--Doctrines--History--Juvenile literature. | Buddhism and culture--Juvenile literature. | World religions--Juvenile literature. | Religious belief--Juvenile literature.
Classification: DDC 294.3--dc23

CONTENTS

HAPPY BIRTHDAY, BUDDHA!

On a warm day in May 2017, the streets of Singapore were alive with delicious smells, joyful sounds, and bright, dazzling decorations. The alleys were full of food carts giving away free snacks to anyone who wanted them. Other vendors brought games and colorful henna plant decorations to the partiers in the streets, and music and singing filled the air. Buildings and alleyways were strung with bright lanterns shaped like lotus flowers, lighting up with bursts of color. The city was hosting a birthday party.

Singapore is an island city-state in southern Asia with 5.6 million citizens.[1] The city welcomes immigrants from many regions. Its religious diversity reflects the Chinese, Malay, Indian, and British influences of its heritage. Singapore has temples and monasteries

Worshippers gather to be blessed on Vesak, which celebrates the Buddha's birthday.

LOTUS

The lotus is a sacred flower in both Hinduism and Buddhism. It is native to Asia and has been a holy symbol for thousands of years. Lotuses can be white or brightly colored. They sit on top of water like lily pads, with their roots in the mud. The lotus is a powerful symbol of rebirth and enlightenment. Lotus flowers grow in muddy water, but then some bloom bright and clean on the water's surface. Because the lotus can spend time in muddy water without getting dirty, it is a symbol of purity as well. Gods, Buddhas, and other powerful people are often portrayed sitting on lotus thrones. Lotus flowers and plants are used in teas and cooking. Lotus flowers are very common in Buddhist art and literature. The lotus lanterns at Vesak are reminders of the flowers that bloomed near the Buddha's feet when he was born.

representing almost all of Buddhism's major traditions. On the full-moon day of the lunar month of Vesakha, usually in spring, people from every faith are invited to celebrate Vesak. It is the birthday of the Buddha, an important teacher in the history of Buddhism.

Vesak is a day of reflection as well as celebration. At Kong Meng San Phor Kark See Monastery on Bright Hill Road, more than 20,000 people came in 2017 to walk barefoot around the temple, taking three steps forward, kneeling, bowing to the ground, and getting up to take another three steps and bow again.[2] Through the night, devotees carried out the three steps, one bow ceremony in turns that lasted more than two hours. Each person focused on letting go of the past, present, and future,

Both monks and lay Buddhists can perform the three steps, one bow ceremony.

Tibetan Buddhists and tourists alike gather to view the beautiful thangkas.

focusing only on the Buddha. Their bows showed respect to the Buddha.

At other temples, people gathered around tubs of water perfumed with flowers. They scooped the water from the basins and poured it over statues of baby Buddha, remembering the bath he was given on his first day on Earth. They brought flowers, incense, and candles to the temples. The gifts were reminders that life passes by quickly, like plucked flowers and burning candles. Monks recited sutras, or holy texts, and visitors to temples could join in chanting as well.

Singapore's Tibetan Buddhist temple follows the tradition of creating and showing a *thangka*, a large sacred picture that can help people with meditation and give blessings to those who see it. In 2017, the temple's thangka was more than four stories high with an image of the sitting Buddha in striking blues and yellows.

Vesak is a day of kindness to animals in the name of the Buddha. Many celebrators give up meat for the day, choosing

to eat a meal of rice in milk similar to a meal the Buddha once ate. It used to be common to free caged birds and other animals on Vesak. Today, Singapore's government cautions people against leaving tame animals to fend for themselves in the wild. People instead show compassion by leaving animals where they're safe and well cared for.

Vesak is also a day for giving gifts. People give gifts to images of the Buddha, to temples, to hungry partiers, and to loved ones and people in need. In Singapore, people come together to give to charity during Vesak. They go to hospitals to donate blood. They visit the less fortunate. In 2016, more than 40 Buddhist temples and 20,000 of their members and visitors joined forces to raise money for Singapore's National Kidney Foundation.[3] They did it to remember the way the Buddha's generosity and compassion touched their lives.

The celebration of Vesak continues well into the night. Thousands of people gather under the full moon and light candles to illuminate their way through the streets, chanting

and singing together. Singapore is not the only place that holds birthday parties for the Buddha. Every spring, there are festivals of music and prayer, statue bathing, and devotion across Asia and on every continent.

What Is Buddhism?

The Buddha was a man who lived in Nepal and northern India more than 2,000 years ago. He was deeply disturbed by the suffering of the world and searched for a way to free himself and others from pain. After many years of meditating and searching, the Buddha found a path out of suffering and into enlightenment. His teachings focus on freeing the self from desire and attachment and avoiding harm to other living beings. He preached his ideas to a community of followers, and their beliefs and practices became the religion known as Buddhism.

Buddhism is a faith practiced by almost 500 million people worldwide. Approximately 7 percent of all people are Buddhists. While there are Buddhists across the world, almost 99 percent live in Asia. Half of all Buddhists live in China, and most of the rest are in East Asia, Southeast Asia, and Tibet.[4]

Buddhism is a complex and diverse religion practiced in many different ways. At its heart, however, Buddhism seeks to end a harmful cycle of death and rebirth by freeing living things from suffering. Buddhists seek to get rid of their illusions about reality and treat others with compassion and wisdom. The life and teachings of the Buddha are their first guides.

BUDDHA STATUES

Statues of the Buddha come in a variety of sizes and shapes—they can be a few inches high or more than 100 feet (30 m) tall.[5] Each type of Buddha statue has a different symbolic meaning expressed in details such as the Buddha's hand positions (known as mudras), his posture, his age, and his facial expression. For example, in some statues, the Buddha is portrayed as having tangled, matted hair, to remind people of the part of his life when he was a wandering seeker.

THE BUDDHA

Buddha is not a given name. It is a title that means "the awakened one" in Sanskrit. The story of the Buddha's life and awakening has been told in thousands of ways. Historians believe that the story of the Buddha dates between 500 and 300 BCE.[1] He was born in or near Lumbini, in what is today southern Nepal. He belonged to a people called the Shakya, who followed a religious and social system with similarities to Hinduism. Similarly to the Hindus of today, the Shakya believed that human beings were reborn after death, living life after life in a series of bodies, in an endless cycle known as samsara.

Shakya society, like many South Asian cultures of the time, organized people into four estates, or social ranks. The second estate, warriors and leaders called the Kshatriya, ruled society. According to traditional biographies, the Buddha was a Kshatriya prince from a royal family named Gautama. However, some historians believe that the Shakya elected their leaders.

The Maya Devi Temple in Nepal marks the place where the Buddha was born.

Tradition says that before coming to Earth, the being who would become the Buddha waited in a heaven, trying to choose the appropriate time and place for his rebirth. His earthly mother, the queen Maya, had a dream about a beautiful white elephant. Shortly after, her son chose to enter her womb. Even his birth was extraordinary. As his mother clung to the branch of a tree for strength, he burst from her right side, dressed in a loincloth, with his hair in a topknot. He walked forward, and lotus flowers began to bloom on the ground his feet touched. Nanda and Upananda, two magical snake kings, came from the sky to bathe and praise the child. His parents named him Siddhartha, meaning "one who reaches his goal." Moments after his birth, baby Siddhartha spoke his first words, announcing this would be his final life. Many stories say Siddhartha's mother died seven days later, leaving him to be raised by his protective father, King Shuddhodana, and his mother's sister.

Shuddhodana saw his son was special. Soon after Siddhartha was born, the king went to astrologers to ask about the boy's future. The seers predicted the prince either would become a world-changing, or "wheel-turning," king or would turn away from the world entirely and become a wandering visionary. Siddhartha's father, eager to have a king for a son, made sure the boy had every advantage and pleasure available at home so he would never want to leave. Young Siddhartha grew up in the comfort and safety of his palace. He was an excellent student, a brilliant archer, and a handsome, sheltered youth.

Entering the Real World

Siddhartha eventually became a man. He married a woman named Gopa and had a son, Rahula. His life was lucky, but he began to sense his ignorance of the outside world. He decided to take a trip to the town outside the palace. Before his son left home, the king made every effort to sweep the area beyond the gates of anything ugly or upsetting, so Siddhartha would see only young and healthy people, happy in their work.

MAYA

Although many traditions say Queen Maya, also known as Mayadevi, died before she could get to know her child, the Buddha and Maya did meet later on. After the Buddha achieved enlightenment, he traveled to a beautiful heaven, the Heaven of the Thirty-Three (also called Tushita), where his mother had been reborn after her death on Earth. There, he taught her and her companions the same lessons he preached on Earth.

appears in many Buddhist fables as a symbol of death, disorder, and the dark side of desire. Mara sent his armies to attack Siddhartha, who sat still and unharmed. Mara also hurled tempting visions, conjuring hallucinations of wealth, power, and beautiful women. But Siddhartha held fast until he arrived at a simple but profound truth.

At last, he understood that the self he had been trying to free from suffering, aging, and death was impossible to save because it did not really exist. It was his attachment to this fake idea of a self that was causing his pain, keeping him inside the endless cycle of aging, sickness, death, and rebirth. Siddhartha had now fully awakened, becoming the Buddha at this moment. He suddenly gained access to memories of eons of his former lives, and he stayed by the tree for seven weeks, absorbing his own enlightenment. In time, the Buddha arose. He was ready to share his message with the world.

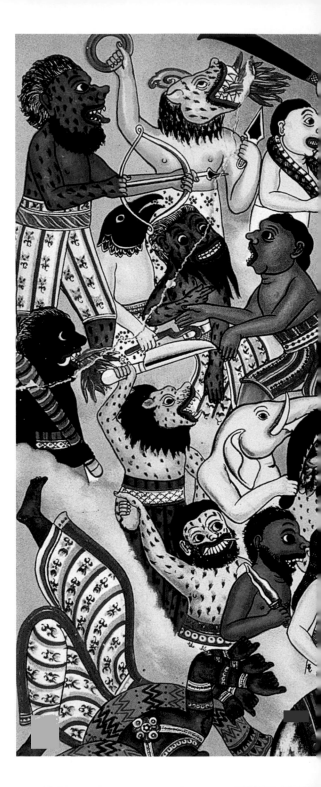

The Buddha's followers listened to his last words of advice before he died.

his followers needed him, but Ananda failed to take the hint and ask his teacher to stay. The Buddha prepared to free himself from existence.

The Buddha asked a blacksmith's son to prepare him a dish of pork and to bury the leftovers when he was finished. The pork was spoiled, and the Buddha's body became sick, experiencing the age and decay that had terrified him so much when he was young. Surrounded by his followers, the Buddha welcomed the end of his life. He passed into nirvana, a state beyond both existence and nonexistence, perception and nonperception. Some Buddhists celebrate this moment each year in February on a holiday known as Parinirvana or Nehan. On it, people visit temples, give gifts, and meditate. Though the Buddha had freed himself from human life, he left behind the dharma as a guide for those who were ready and willing to follow his path.

THE DHARMA: BELIEFS AND PRACTICES

The Buddha gave his followers a cure for suffering. To understand his solution, it is necessary to understand the problem itself. Buddhists see themselves as part of a large and complicated universe with many worlds beyond this one. The universe runs according to a law called karma, which affects the fate of all living beings. Beyond life, death, and karma, there is nirvana, the state that extinguishes all existence and is the final Buddhist goal.

Buddhism teaches that there are many worlds and possibly many universes. Death and rebirth do not only occur on Earth. There are heavens and hells with gods and demons living in them. After death, human beings can die and be reborn into a heaven. They spend varying amounts of time there, from brief stays to many eons,

For Buddhists, lighting lanterns is symbolic of lighting the way to enlightenment.

THE CREATION OF THE UNIVERSE

According to traditional Buddhist thought, the origin of the universe is impossible to understand. However, one Buddhist story of the universe's creation tells of a group of beings with see-through bodies who came to this realm after their old one was destroyed. They were attracted to the material of the universe and started to eat it as food. Soon, the universe food turned them into beings with solid bodies and strong material desires, and they began to fight each other out of greed and hunger.

before possibly coming back to Earth. Buddhist literature often describes heavens as stunningly beautiful, full of jewels, beautiful music, sweet smells, and lotus flowers. For example, the Heaven of the Thirty-Three, where Maya went after her death, was famous as the home of many powerful Indian gods.

Types of Rebirth

The cycle of death and rebirth includes more than just humans on Earth. Beings can be reborn as gods, demigods, humans, animals, ghosts, and hell beings. Buddhist gods and demigods are powerful, but they are not immortal. They can live for thousands, possibly millions, of years.

It is lucky to be reborn as a human, although of course some humans are luckier than others. Rebirth as an animal is not as lucky, since many animals live short, anxious, and painful lives. Animals also usually do not have the mental ability to work toward enlightenment. Ghosts are even less fortunate than animals. They are trapped in a world that cannot see them, with cravings and desires they can never satisfy. Ghosts are often described as hungry, with huge bellies and tiny mouths, desperate for food they are unable to eat. Even existence as a ghost, however, may be better than rebirth into a hell. There are plenty of Buddhist hells, just as there are many Buddhist heavens. There are hot hells and cold hells. There are sections of hells reserved for specific types of wrong actions, such as cheating on a spouse or killing birds for no reason.

There have also been other Buddhas in different eras and realms. Siddhartha Gautama is the Buddha people on Earth know best, but Buddhist tradition has identified

A monastery in Thailand made a hell garden full of depictions of creatures and punishments one might face in a hell.

judge who watches people's choices and decides their karma. Instead, the chain of action and consequences happens naturally and inevitably. Being born wealthy or lucky is seen as a sign of good karma in a past life. Negative life events such as losses and natural disasters may be the result of harmful actions in the past.

Not all actions are equally important as far as karma is concerned. Sometimes one small action from a long-ago life can have a large effect, either painful or happy, in a future life. A person's intentions and state of mind at the time of death are especially important in determining the fate of that person's future lives.

Since karma is such a powerful force, it might seem that the goal of every Buddhist should be to do as many good deeds as possible to enjoy rebirth in a heaven. However, the Buddha was skeptical of all types of karma. He believed joy and excitement could be just as dangerous as pain, since they both represent forms of attachment to existence and samsara.

Many Buddhists meditate while sitting cross-legged and keeping their spines straight.

The Buddha told a famous story about people who worried too much about the nature of nirvana. They put off their journey to enlightenment until they knew their destination. He compared those people to a man who had been shot by a poison arrow and wanted to know everything about the arrow—who had shot it, why he had been attacked, what kind of poison was on the tip, at what angle it had entered his body—before he even tried to save his life by pulling the arrow out. The Buddha encouraged his followers to remove the arrow first and find answers later.

THE WHEEL OF DHARMA: CHANGES AND SPREAD

In the centuries after the Buddha's death, traveling merchants, missionary monks, and shifting cultural trends helped spread Buddhism across Asia. Buddhism changed a great deal as it moved through space and time. Through hundreds of years, the Buddha's original message developed into three major schools of Buddhist thought. They are the Theravada, Mahayana, and Vajrayana schools, known in their original languages as "vehicles" because they turn the wheel of the dharma in the world. Each of these three schools is most popular and influential in a different part of Asia.

Theravada monks carefully study the Pali Canon, which they believe is the most accurate record of the Buddha's teachings.

ASHVAGHOSHA

Ashvaghosha is known as one of the first and most important Buddhist poets. He was born in approximately 100 BCE in northern India. Legends say he became a Buddhist as an adult after losing an argument to a Buddhist scholar. In addition to his great work of Mahayana philosophy, *The Awakening of the Faith*, he is famous for a poetic biography of the Buddha. He may also have played a role in organizing one of the first Buddhist councils, where monks from various Buddhist lands gathered to recite and write down important texts.

This form of Buddhism is called *Mahayana*, sometimes interpreted as the "Great Vehicle," where *great* means "all-encompassing." Mahayana Buddhism encourages all followers to recognize and work toward their own inborn potential for Buddhahood. While other schools of Buddhism share the idea of the bodhisattva, it is an especially important Mahayana ideal. Bodhisattvas often have supernatural powers, and other Buddhists can call on them for help. One famous bodhisattva is Avalokiteshvara, also known in Chinese as Guanyin. Avalokiteshvara, known as the bodhisattva of compassion, is sometimes described as male and sometimes appears as female. People can recite his verse in a famous text called the Lotus Sutra for his protection from "flood, shipwreck, murderers, demons, prison, bandits, and wild animals."[3] This bodhisattva is also known in China as a white-robed god who can give sons to infertile people.

In addition to its focus on compassion and helping others, Mahayana Buddhist philosophy also discusses the emptiness and illusions of existence. Some Mahayana scholars believe the Buddha had a spiritual as well as a physical body, or that what appeared to be the Buddha's body was just an illusion the spiritual Buddha presented. Others extended this idea to understand that the whole universe was nothing but the body of the Buddha himself. Nirvana was not a goal, but an existing, eternal state of being.

Mahayana philosophers often discussed the idea of emptiness. There was no difference between

A Buddha statue sits in the Mahayana Buddhist Temple in New York City, New York.

THE DALAI LAMA

In 1933, the thirteenth Dalai Lama, a powerful political leader who led a movement to modernize an independent Tibet, died. In 1935, the fourteenth Dalai Lama was born in a small Tibetan farming village. Lhamo Thondup was recognized as an incarnate lama at age two and became a novice monk at age six. Tibet has had a violent and complicated political history. The Dalai Lama's destiny was to become Tibet's political and spiritual leader. But in 1959, he had to flee the country after a Tibetan uprising against the Chinese government, which administers Tibet as part of its territory. The Dalai Lama has lived in exile ever since. In 1989, the Dalai Lama won the Nobel Peace Prize for his efforts on behalf of world peace and Tibetan independence. He travels the world giving lectures, educating others about Buddhism, and advocating on behalf of a variety of causes. He has met with dozens of heads of state and has written more than 100 books. In 2011, the Dalai Lama stepped down as Tibet's political leader so Tibetans could form a more democratic government.

Tibetan Buddhist teachers are known as lamas. In Tibet, after an especially great lama dies, his followers try to find him in his next rebirth. The reborn lama, a young boy, is trained to become a teacher himself and carry on the tradition of his past life. These reborn lamas have a great deal of power in Tibetan culture. The most famous incarnate lama is the fourteenth Dalai Lama, born in 1935. He is considered the rebirth of a great teacher who died in 1474. Followers consider the Dalai Lama a

The Dalai Lama has spoken around the world.

manifestation of Avalokiteshvara. Since 1642, Dalai Lamas have served on and off as the political and religious leaders of Tibet.

The lamas of Tibet are just one part of the vast and rich tradition of the sangha, or community of Buddhist monks and nuns. This community follows a variety of paths. It makes up the third jewel of Buddhism.

Many monks today still rely on food donations.

CHAPTER FIVE

THE SANGHA

When the Buddha began to live with a community of followers, it made sense for the group to live like those of their time who practiced self-denial. They wore simple robes, often castoffs or hand-me-downs, and they shaved their heads to show they did not care about physical appearances. They carried wooden bowls with them to collect food donations from nonmonks and used fermented cow urine as medicine for their sicknesses. The gifts of food they received from sympathetic people, as well as other charitable gifts that helped them live, are known as alms.

The monks' spare lifestyles became harder to maintain as the number of the Buddha's followers grew. Monks began to settle in permanent communities instead of wandering the countryside and sleeping outdoors. Monastic communities realized they needed a set of rules, or vows, for proper monk behavior. These rules are known as the Five Precepts. Buddhists in Southeast Asia celebrate the day the Buddha gave his followers rules for monastic life on Magha Puja,

ordination ceremony where Thai monks promise to keep 227 vows, monastic life begins.[1]

In one Thai monastery, monks wake at 4:00 a.m. Before breakfast, many monks go on an alms round, walking miles from the monastery into a nearby town with their bowls, collecting food and other donations. Many Thai monks are not allowed to handle money, so the alms they collect are mostly in the form of food (cooked especially for them) or useful gifts. Breakfast is at 6:00 a.m. Afterward, monks, visitors, and mae chee either chant and meditate or take care of the chores of the order. At 10:30 a.m., everyone eats lunch. Since monastery residents have vowed not to eat food after noon, this lunch is the last meal of the day. Between 3:00 and 6:00 p.m., the monks may meet with a meditation teacher to discuss their own progress. At 5:00 p.m., there is another hour and a half of chanting. Once a week at 8:00 p.m., the community gathers to chant, discuss problems, and hear lectures. In the

PERSPECTIVES

JEONG KWAN, NUN AND MASTER CHEF

Since the age of 17, Jeong Kwan has lived as a nun in a Zen monastery in South Korea. She prepares meals for other monks and nuns. Her meals have become world famous for their simplicity, taste, and respect for nature. Jeong Kwan grows food in her own garden and believes that her connection with the plants improves the quality of her food. She keeps a garden without walls that grows in and out of the nearby forest, and she doesn't prevent insects or pests from eating her plants if they choose. Her motto is "Let nature take care of it."[6] She prepares meals without meat, dairy, fish, and the five strong flavors, including garlic and onions. Her cooking focuses on the Buddhist principles of eliminating desire and clarifying the mind.

Jeong Kwan takes time to prepare food in nature, using the ground to ferment kimchi, a pickled food made with traditional Korean cabbage, and letting some of her sauces age for years before they are ready. Jeong Kwan believes she may have been a cook in a former life. She says, "There is no difference between cooking and pursuing Buddha's way. . . . I am not a chef, I am a monk."[7]

wandering monks and forest monks who keep a simpler life farther away from society.

Buddhist Nuns

Since the beginning of Buddhism, there have been Buddhist nuns. A nun's vows are different from a monk's. When the Buddha allowed women to become nuns, he also put a series of eight rules in place that restricted nuns' freedoms and privileges. For example, nun ordination vows say that while monks can criticize nuns, nuns cannot criticize monks. These are known as the eight "heavy rules," or *garudhamma*. Furthermore, ten fully ordained nuns have to be in the room when a new nun is ordained.[5] This practice has caused the nun tradition to die out in many places because there are too few nuns available to carry it on. Most fully ordained Buddhist nuns live in

Nuns in some areas wear different colors than monks.

East Asia. In fact, in Taiwan, there are more Buddhist nuns than monks. Yet in many parts of the world, such as in Theravada Thai monasteries, women who live religious lives lack all the privileges of nuns. However, this is changing in some places. In 2017, the seventeenth Karmapa, a great teacher of Tibet, made it possible for Tibetan women to take their vows to be fully ordained nuns.

SHAOLIN TEMPLE

The Shaolin Temple is a Zen monastery in Henan province in central China. It is famous worldwide as the home of Shaolin kung fu, an ancient martial art that combines the mental discipline of Zen Buddhism with Chinese fighting techniques. Legend says that the Indian monk Bodhidharma founded the monastery when he came to China in approximately 500 CE. His statue still stands there.

The temple became world famous in the 1900s thanks to a series of action movies. One movie, 1982's *The Shaolin Temple*, is based on an ancient legend. It stars Chinese actor Jet Li as a young man who learns kung fu from the temple monks to take revenge on the unjust king who killed his father.

In real life, the monks of Shaolin Temple do practice their own several-hundred-year-old tradition of kung fu and teach it to visitors. The monastery has always been wealthy, but lately its earnings have exploded as the Shaolin brand of temples expands to North America and Europe. The abbot of Shaolin, Shi Yongxin, is a controversial figure, with some people criticizing what they see as his greed and hypocrisy. Shaolin Temple's seeming contradictions help show the richness and complexity of Buddhist experience.

THE SANGHA AND THE COMMUNITY

The sangha is a vital part of the Buddhist religion. But the Buddhist world stretches far beyond its monasteries and temples. Throughout Buddhist history, most Buddhists have not been monks or nuns. Instead, they have been kings, queens, artists, farmers, pirates, craftspeople, and human beings from every possible walk of life. The sangha plays many important roles in the relationship between Buddhist tradition and nonmonastic, or lay, Buddhists. Monasteries and temples are usually linked, so Buddhists who come to see relics or make offerings at temples will come into contact with the monks who maintain them. The stupas, statues, relics, and art that monasteries preserve are vital for community worship.

Buddhists may go to the temple to pray or request help.

Traditionally, monks do not perform marriages or involve themselves much in weddings, although they might bless a couple after a marriage ceremony. However, the sangha does play a large role in funeral ceremonies. Monks may recite sutras for the dead and perform rituals that help the deceased avoid a bad rebirth. Japanese Buddhism even has a tradition of ordaining dead bodies as monks, shaving their heads and reciting vows so they can possibly have a better rebirth. Tibetan Buddhists believe that dead people spend time in a bardo, or space between worlds, before being reborn. The bardo can be a confusing and overwhelming place. The texts and Tantras of Tibetan monks teach people how to move through it to the next life.

STUPA

A stupa is a Buddhist shrine traditionally shaped like a dome. Stupas are built to contain relics—parts of the Buddha's body or other possessions. Stupas can also have relics of other Buddhist gods, bodhisattvas, or great monks. At temples and monasteries, people visit stupas to get close to the relics and make merit. There are famous stupas at the Mahabodhi Temple in India, built at the site of the bodhi tree where the Buddha was enlightened.

Merit and the Sangha

Buddhists are concerned with making merit, or doing things that produce good karma for a better future rebirth. Monasteries can act like factories for merit, helping people give donations or perform religious acts that build merit in their lives.

For lay Buddhists, donating food, money, or land to a monastery can be a powerful form of giving with effects in other lives. In Southeast Asia,

THE *TIBETAN BOOK OF THE DEAD*

There is a famous Tibetan text called *The Great Liberation through Hearing in the Intermediate State*, or *Bardo Thödol*. It is thought to have been written in the 700s CE. The text gives instructions on how to navigate the sights, sounds, and feelings of the first stages of death. It also tells how to move through the bardo on the way to a good rebirth. It is famous for its vivid descriptions of the visions of the bardo. It reminds the dead not to panic at the frightening animals, gods, and spirits they might see there. *Bardo Thödol* is meant to be read to people who have just died so they can hear the lessons on how to move to the next life. In English, this book has become known as the *Tibetan Book of the Dead* and has been translated several times. It is a fascinating but incomplete look at Tibetan ideas about death and rebirth.

where many monks rely on alms for their food, the almsgivers can increase their own merit by giving regularly to the monks. Many monks are not allowed to turn down extra or unwanted food because refusing the gift would prevent the giver from making merit.

Monasteries often store collections of sutras and other holy texts and teach their monks how to read and recite them. Historically, monks have been some of the most educated and well-read people in Buddhist societies. Lay Buddhists can enlist monks' special skills and knowledge for themselves by making donations for a certain number of prayers. Reciting sutras on another person's behalf can bring that person protection and power and helps that person build merit, and laypeople can

> ## TEMPLE AND MONASTERY ANIMALS
>
> People have traditionally brought abandoned animals to Buddhist temples. Monks and nuns care for these animals, which may include stray cats, dogs, and even monkeys. Monks, inspired by their vow of ahimsa, care for these homeless animals, which become part of temple life. However, some temples receive so many animals they can no longer take good care of all of them.

ask monks to perform recitations or copy sutras for themselves or loved ones.

Some monasteries are closed off to the outside world except on certain ritual days or holidays. For example, many South Korean monasteries are mostly closed to the public except on Vesak, when they serve free vegetarian lunches to visitors and celebrate with lotus lanterns and baths for the Buddha statues. These holidays can be some of the only times for lay Buddhists to see the workings of a monastery up close, and they are important opportunities for lay worshippers to gain merit through observance and ritual.

Monks and Society

Monks are often educated, well connected, and wise. As a result, they are sometimes very powerful. Many times throughout history, monks have served as advisers to kings and rulers who relied on their wisdom and presumed supernatural powers. Some monasteries became powerful institutions with

Buddhists can make merit by burning incense for the Buddha.

A vegetarian meal at a temple might include noodles, a variety of vegetables, and tofu.

the ability to hire their own soldiers. In Japan, Buddhist monks quickly became very powerful because Japanese rulers thought their magical abilities could bring safety and good fortune to the state.

Not every Buddhist has had a positive view of monks. Some people have seen monks as men who are too lazy or immature to survive in the real world. There are stories of corrupt monasteries full of

MONK MARRIAGE IN JAPAN

In 1872, the Meiji government of Japan announced that monks would be allowed to marry, eat meat, grow their hair, and break other traditional monastic laws. Previously, the government had helped Buddhists enforce traditional rules by punishing members of the sangha who broke them. However, at the time, the Japanese government wanted to modernize the country and reduce the influence of religious law. Many Buddhists were upset by the government's action, which they felt took power away from Buddhist institutions and left Buddhists less able to enforce their traditions. Since then, Japanese monks have been able to marry and have children. Many small Buddhist monasteries are passed on from fathers to sons. Wives help run the temple, and some are even priests.

fun-loving monks who do not have to work for a living and spend their days gambling and drinking. In some places, it has not been uncommon for monks to have children, even though they are not supposed to marry or have sex. There are regions where monasteries developed reputations as hiding places for people who were fleeing past crimes. Nevertheless, for the Buddhist community as a whole, the sangha serves an irreplaceable role. Buddhists who cannot or do not want to live as monks or nuns in this life can still use the monastery as a tool to gain wisdom and improve their rebirth.

BUDDHISM AND THE WEST

The Italian explorer Marco Polo traveled to Asia along the Silk Road in the late 1200s. This road was actually an ancient series of trade routes through western and central Asia. Merchants could travel and exchange goods such as spices, silk and other textiles, and wood and metal crafts. When Polo visited China, he learned about the Mahayana Buddhism that had existed there for more than 1,000 years. Polo, who thought about Buddhism from his own medieval Catholic perspective, described the Buddha as a man who would have been a saint if he had been born a Christian. Polo may not have understood Buddhism well, but most Europeans of his time had never heard of it at all.

Even so, communication along the Silk Road helped information travel in unexpected ways. There is a medieval Christian story called

Marco Polo recorded his journeys in a book called *The Travels of Marco Polo*, which also contained illustrations.

"Barlaam and Josaphaat" that is actually a retelling of the Buddha's story. Most Europeans would have never guessed that the word *Josaphaat* was originally *bodhisattva*.

By the 1800s, some European countries, especially the United Kingdom and France, had conquered large parts of South and Southeast Asia and hoped to gain more political control in China and Japan. European colonizers became curious about Buddhism and Buddhist culture. Around this time, British scholars translated the Pali Canon. They began the Pali Text Society, which was devoted to studying Buddhist writings. These people, part of a group of scholars called Orientalists, published their research for other Westerners and helped build Western awareness of Buddhism. English Victorians called Theosophists, who were interested in magic, séances, and communication with spirits, became fascinated by Hinduism and Buddhism, popularizing their own versions of Buddhist texts and beliefs.

THE SILK ROAD AND WEST ASIAN BUDDHISM

More than 1,000 years ago, Buddhism was a thriving religion in Afghanistan and Pakistan. The Silk Road helped Buddhism travel west from India to West Asia. In the 500s, people in the ancient Buddhist city of Bamiyan, Afghanistan, constructed two standing Buddha statues, each more than 100 feet (30 m) high, in the rock valley near their city.[1] The Taliban, a political and religious group, destroyed the statues in 2001. But beautiful and ancient West Asian cave temples remain as proof of Buddhist influence in the region.

Growth of Western Buddhism

Some of the first Buddhists in the United States were Chinese immigrants to the West Coast in the mid-1800s. Japanese immigrants followed them, establishing new Buddhist temples and meeting places. Other Asian immigrants also brought their Buddhist beliefs and practices with them to the United States. In 1893, visitors to the World's Parliament of Religions in Chicago, Illinois, could meet and learn from Buddhist representatives. Some Americans were introduced to Buddhist thought for the first time when Buddhists from Japan discussed their religion. In the late 1800s and early 1900s, however, the United States restricted the number of Asian immigrants allowed in the country, preventing many Buddhists from settling. In the 1940s, the incarceration of 120,000 Japanese Americans during World War II (1939–1945), as well as government surveillance of Buddhist leaders, deeply hurt the size and safety of the American Buddhist community.

ORIENTALISM

The word *Orient* is an old Western term for Asia and the Middle East. The term *Orientalist* was first used to describe Western scholars and researchers who studied Asian and Middle Eastern languages and cultures. However, in 1978, the Palestinian thinker Edward Said published a book that argued that Orientalists used negative and ignorant stereotypes about the East in their research. He believed Orientalists used their studies as a way to gain power over other cultures. Said changed the way many people look at religious and cultural studies.

Buddhism quickly gained popularity in the West in the 1950s and 1960s. The United States became involved with conflicts in Korea and Vietnam, countries with large Buddhist populations.

COUNTERCULTURE

In the 1950s and 1960s, people opposed to the values and activities of modern Western life started to define themselves as part of a counterculture. This counterculture was a way of life that went against the mainstream. Members of the counterculture pursued new trends in music, clothing, and art. They sometimes experimented with hallucinogenic drugs and new kinds of romantic relationships. They were often fascinated by Asian cultures, and other South and East Asian religions also became more popular in the West around this time. Members of countercultures were sometimes called "hippies," "peaceniks," or "Beats."

Many people came together to protest US involvement in the Vietnam War and American aggression in a majority-Buddhist country. The Vietnamese monk Thich Nhat Hanh, an outspoken anti-war voice, came to the United States in the 1960s and attracted supporters and admirers. Civil rights hero Martin Luther King Jr. nominated Hanh for the Nobel Peace Prize for his work connecting the Vietnamese struggle to other fights for independence and civil rights worldwide.

During this time, many Westerners were drawn to Buddhism because of what they saw as its peacefulness and focus outside the self. Young people in European and North American countries began to question the traditional values they had learned as children. They were dissatisfied by what they saw as the greed, individualism, and violence of Western culture and wanted to explore other paths. America's first Buddhist monasteries, Buddhist seminaries, and centers for Buddhist studies all opened in the 1960s. D. T. Suzuki, a Japanese Buddhist who had lived on and off in the United States for more than 50 years, helped introduce Zen Buddhism to the United States. He is partly responsible for the large influence of Zen on Western Buddhism.

Buddhists also began to have a larger presence in American and European arts and culture. In the 1950s and 1960s, famous writers such as Allen Ginsberg, Jack Kerouac, and Alan Watts wrote books and poems inspired by Buddhist ideas. Americans and Europeans made pilgrimages to monasteries across

PERSPECTIVES

THICH QUANG DUC PROTESTS

On a June day in 1963, during a protest on a busy street in Saigon, Vietnam, a Mahayana monk sat down in the middle of an intersection. With the help of two other monks, he let himself be doused in kerosene and set himself on fire.

Thich Quang Duc was protesting the mistreatment of Buddhists by the Vietnamese government, then led by President Ngo Dinh Diem, a Catholic. In a letter Duc wrote shortly before he died, he said, "Before closing my eyes and moving toward the vision of the Buddha, I respectfully plead to President Diem to take a mind of compassion toward the people of the nation and implement religious equality to maintain the strength of the homeland eternally. I call the venerables, reverends, members of the sangha and the lay Buddhists to organize in solidarity to make sacrifices to protect Buddhism."[2]

The moment of Duc's death was captured in a shocking photograph that quickly appeared in newspapers worldwide. President Diem was overthrown later that year, but Vietnam descended into more than a decade of war and violence. In the later years of conflict in Vietnam, many other monks followed in Duc's footsteps, and the tactic spread to other parts of the world.

There are Buddhist temples across the United States. The Byodu-In Temple is on the Hawaiian island Oahu.

Asia, including in Tibet, to learn directly from members of the sangha.

Western Buddhism Today

The counterculture poets, protesters, and seekers who first embraced Buddhism in the West were looking for a way to protest what they saw as harmful parts of Western society. But these days, the focus has shifted. Today, many Buddhists and seekers are more focused on finding ways to blend Western and Buddhist ideas together.

Although the first Buddhists in the West were Asian immigrants, today most Western Buddhists are converts from other cultures and traditions. Western Buddhists tend to be more focused on meditation than nonmonastic Buddhists in other countries. In recent years, Western Buddhists have tried to make connections between the mental effects of Buddhist meditation and Western scientific ideas about thinking and the brain. Some Westerners believe that the Buddhist idea that there is no self is compatible with Western cognitive science.

BUDDHISM AND THEORIES OF EVOLUTION

Robert Wright, an American journalist and professor, wrote a book called *Why Buddhism Is True*. In the book, he argues that the Buddha's teachings can be proven correct by comparing them with scientific evolutionary theories about how the mind works. For instance, Wright says that evolution has created the human brain to be anxious and worried because those are the traits that help people stay alive in dangerous situations. According to Wright, Buddhism recognizes this truth about the human brain and can help people overcome it through meditation.

Wright's argument is an example of the intersection between Western scientific ideas and Buddhist thought. On the one hand, Wright has a great deal of respect for Buddhist ideals and meditates regularly. On the other hand, his argument implies Buddhist spirituality is acceptable or true only if it agrees with current Western ideas about how brains and bodies work.

Others, including neuroscientist Richard Davidson, are investigating whether learning the Buddhist values of compassion and generosity prompt the brain to respond with happiness. Popular meditation centers, meditation podcasts, and meditation apps promote Buddhist ideas of no self and right mindfulness alongside other goals such as productivity and inner calm.

Buddhism's journey in the West demonstrates how the religion has changed and been changed by every culture it has touched. Globalization continues to connect Buddhists across the world. Western Buddhists will continue to add their interpretations and perspectives to the layers of Buddhist thought.

Temples in the United States may serve both as places of worship and as places where people can learn about Buddhism and the cultures in which it is often practiced.

CHALLENGES

As with any ancient and diverse tradition, Buddhism can be difficult to understand. Believers and nonbelievers argue about the meanings of its writings, practices, beliefs, and history. Buddhism's relationship to violence and its understanding of the role of women are topics of especially intense debate. Additionally, people outside the faith often misunderstand the role of meditation in Buddhism and the status of Buddhism as a world religion.

Buddhism, War, and Peace

The satirical website the Onion once published a fake article with the headline "Buddhist Extremist Cell Vows to Unleash Tranquility on West."[1] The article made a joke about the fact that the news often seems to be full of stories about extremist religious groups that wage war and cause destruction in the name of God. Buddhism's commitment to nonviolence makes the idea of Buddhist terrorism seem ridiculous and unrealistic. The joke reveals that there is a

Generalizing a religion that millions of people follow can lead to stereotyping.

stereotype of Buddhists as unusually peaceful, passive, and maybe even boring. Like all stereotypes, this one is a distortion of the full truth.

It's true that many Buddhists take the principle of ahimsa seriously and are careful not to cause unnecessary pain to other living beings. However, there are many ways to interpret Buddhist ideas about right action and right livelihood. Buddhists throughout history have planned and participated in wars. There have been long traditions of warrior monks in Buddhism. Some of these monks fought on behalf of the kingdoms or regions they lived in, and others went to war for their monasteries, which were sometimes very wealthy and powerful places. Buddhist literature contains descriptions of battles, killing, and war among both gods and humans. Buddhist thought also says that people who live in the world must try to become successful according to the laws and customs of their own societies. For ordinary people, this can mean defending themselves and their possessions with violence. For governments and empires, the same logic can apply.

It is also important to remember that Buddhists, like all human beings, do not always live according to the laws of their religion or follow their highest moral values. One example of the complex relationship between Buddhism and violence is the current human rights crisis in the Southeast Asian nation of Burma, a majority-Buddhist country with a small Muslim minority. The government is expelling Rohingya Muslims from their homes, condoning or directing rape and murder, and burning villages and towns. Its actions have the full support and participation of many

Many Rohingya have fled Burma, bringing along only what they can carry.

Burmese Buddhists, including monks. Between late August 2016 and October 2017, more than 600,000 Rohingya Muslims had fled their homes.[2] Many devout Buddhists support the violence, claiming that Rohingya, and Muslims in general, are lesser people and do not belong in Burma. One Buddhist monk even thanked the "Lord Buddha" for the killings and displacement.[3]

Women in Buddhism

Tradition says that even though the Buddha welcomed male followers, he was reluctant to allow women to become part of the sangha as well. His companion Ananda pointed out that the former wives of monks had been abandoned by their husbands and needed their own community to live in. Finally, the Buddha agreed to Ananda's request and allowed women to become nuns, although he complained that allowing women into the sangha would make his preaching less effective.

This story helps show some contradictions about the role of women in Buddhism. On the one hand, women have been included in Buddhist life since the beginning of the religion. On the other hand, Buddhist monks have more power and freedom than Buddhist nuns. Buddhist philosophy and mythology have positive portrayals of women and female figures, but they also show signs of misogyny, the hatred of women or belief that women are inferior to men. For example, the Buddha's

Some Taiwanese nuns are activists protesting government activities they see as dangerous, such as operating nuclear power plants.

mother, Maya, is an honored and respected figure, residing in a heaven after an excellent life on Earth. However, some scholars believe the reason the Buddha is described as being born from his mother's side is because early Buddhists believed natural birth from a woman was disgusting and unworthy of respect. Some sources even say Maya's womb was transformed into a bejeweled palace during the Buddha's stay there, because the unborn baby was too noble to suffer the uncleanliness of a normal

BUDDHISM WORLDWIDE

In the 1900s, technology and shifts in global politics changed Buddhism's relationship with the world. Today, there are many ways for Buddhists to connect with each other across national and cultural barriers. The World Buddhist Directory, run by the organization BuddhaNet, keeps a record of Buddhist organizations sorted by location and tradition. There are international organizations and conferences for Buddhist members of the sangha, scholars of Buddhism, and Buddhists concerned about global issues such as social justice and climate change. In 1950, the World Federation of Buddhists officially adopted a six-stripe Buddhist flag. The flag is often used to celebrate Buddhist national holidays.

Sacred Buddhist sites such as the birthplace of the Buddha in Lumbini and the site of Buddha's enlightenment have been recognized by the United Nations as World Heritage Sites, vital places

The colors on the Buddhist flag represent the colors that shone from the Buddha when he reached enlightenment.

The Zen garden in Ryoanji Temple is one of the most famous gardens.

literature, tells the tale of a traveling Buddhist monk. It has been the inspiration for operas, plays, movies, anime, manga, and even video games. Buddhist cuisine has a long and deep tradition. In Chinese cooking, vegetarian meals such as Buddha's Delight, a dish with cabbage and tofu, were designed for people who took the vow of ahimsa, either permanently or temporarily. Many other Asian cuisines make similar dishes for Buddhist holidays and celebrations.

Outside of individual monasteries, Buddhism has never had an official leadership structure. There is no head Buddhist, and the influence of global Buddhist conferences is limited. But like the bodhisattvas and great teachers of history, there are Buddhists today who have become role models and international celebrities. In 1985, American astronaut Ellison Onizuka became the first Buddhist to fly in space. The Dalai Lama is probably the world's most famous Buddhist, and Thich Nhat Hanh also has a large global following. In the 2000s and 2010s, Buddhist artists such as Leonard Cohen, Tina Turner, Jet

Devotees and tourists alike visit temples to pray and learn more about Buddhism.

world has grown and shifted in countless ways that would have been impossible for its first followers to predict. There will be other changes in the future. But throughout the inevitable upheavals of samsara, the core messages of Buddhism remain ready for discovery by anyone who looks for them.

ESSENTIAL FACTS

DATE FOUNDED

Buddhism was founded in approximately 500 BCE.

BASIC BELIEFS

Human beings exist in a cycle of birth, death, and rebirth that is defined by suffering and pain. People can achieve enlightenment and find a state known as nirvana, the end of all suffering. Buddhists follow the Buddha by cultivating wisdom and showing compassion and generosity to others. They do good deeds and live morally to have good karma for future lives, and they meditate, recite texts, and visit holy places to draw closer to enlightenment and nirvana.

IMPORTANT HOLIDAYS AND EVENTS

- Many Buddhists celebrate Vesak, the Buddha's birthday, in the spring.

- Magha Puja, also known as Sangha Day, is a day devoted to good deeds and making merit. It commemorates the day when the Buddha first gave the rules for the sangha. Buddhists in Southeast Asia celebrate it in late February or early March.

- Parinirvana, also known as Nehan, is a Mahayana holiday that celebrates the day the Buddha died and achieved nirvana. Parinirvana is a day of visiting temples and bringing them presents, and it is a day of meditation.

FAITH LEADERS

⊙ The Dalai Lama, a Tibetan monk

⊙ Thich Nhat Hanh, a Vietnamese monk

NUMBER OF PEOPLE WHO PRACTICE BUDDHISM

There are almost 500 million Buddhists living today. Approximately 99 percent of Buddhists live in Asia.

QUOTE

"Meditation is about the awareness of what is going on—not only in your body and in your feelings, but all around you."

—Thich Nhat Hanh

ADDITIONAL RESOURCES

SELECTED BIBLIOGRAPHY

Keown, Damien. *Buddhism: A Very Short Introduction*. Oxford, UK: Oxford UP, 2013. Print.

Lopez, Donald S., Jr. *The Story of Buddhism: A Concise Guide to Its History and Teachings*. San Francisco, CA: HarperSanFrancisco, 2001. Print.

Roebuck, Valerie J. *The Dhammapada*. New York: Penguin, 2010. Print.

FURTHER READINGS

McFarlane, Marilyn. *Sacred Stories: Wisdom from World Religions*. New York: Beyond Words, 2012. Print.

Rowell, Rebecca. *Ancient India*. Minneapolis: Abdo, 2015. Print.

ONLINE RESOURCES

To learn more about Buddhism, visit **abdobooklinks.com**. These links are routinely monitored and updated to provide the most current information available.

MORE INFORMATION

For more information on this subject, contact or visit the following organizations:

DEER PARK MONASTERY

2499 Melru Lane
Escondido, CA 92026
760-291-1003
deerparkmonastery.org

This Buddhist monastery, founded by Thich Nhat Hanh, offers retreats and day visits as well as information on mindfulness.

SHAMBHALA MEDITATION CENTER OF NEW YORK

118 W. Twenty-Second Street, Sixth Floor
New York, NY 10011
212-675-6544
ny.shambhala.org

Shambhala Meditation Center holds meditation classes and lectures on Buddhist teachings.

SOURCE NOTES

Chapter 1. Happy Birthday, Buddha!

1. "Singapore." *One World Nations Online.* Nationsonline.org, 2018. Web. 23 Feb. 2018.

2. Ng Wei Kai. "Thousands Turn Up at Temple for Rituals ahead of Vesak Day." *The Straights Times Singapore.* Singapore Press Holdings, 10 May 2017. Web. 23 Feb. 2018.

3. "Vesak Day Charity Drive 2016." *NKF.* National Kidney Foundation, n.d. Web. 23 Feb. 2018.

4. "Buddhists." *Pew Research Center: Religion & Public Life.* Pew Research Center, 18 Dec. 2012. Web. 23 Feb. 2018.

5. "Giant Buddha Statues." *World Heritage Sites.* WHS, 2018. Web. 23 Feb. 2018.

Chapter 2. The Buddha

1. Donald S. Lopez. "Buddha." *Encyclopædia Britannica.* Encyclopædia Britannica, 2 Feb. 2018. Web. 23 Feb. 2018.

2. Donald S. Lopez. *The Story of Buddhism: A Concise Guide to Its History and Teaching.* San Francisco: Harper, 2001. Print. 54–56.

Chapter 3. The Dharma: Beliefs and Practices

None.

Chapter 4. The Wheel of Dharma: Changes and Spread

1. F. Max Müller. *Wisdom of the Buddha: The Unabridged Dhammapada*. Mineola, NY: Dover, 2000. Print. 34.

2. Donald S. Lopez. *The Story of Buddhism: A Concise Guide to Its History and Teaching*. San Francisco: Harper, 2001. Print. 54–56.

3. Lopez, *The Story of Buddhism*, 80.

4. Teitaro Suzuki, trans., *The Awakening of Faith: The Classic Exposition of Mahayana Buddhism*. Dover ed. Mineola, NY: Dover, 2003. Print. 74.

5. Donald S. Lopez Jr., ed., *Buddhism in Practice*. Abridged ed. Princeton, NJ: Princeton UP, 2007. 90–91. *Google Books*. Web. 23 Feb. 2018.

6. Edward Conze. *Buddhism: Its Essence and Development, Etc.* Faber & Faber, 1963. Print. 202.

7. Kazuaki Tanahashi and John Daido Loori, trans., *The True Dharma Eye: Zen Master Dogen's Three Hundred Koans*. Boston: Shambhala, 2005. 231. Web. *Google Books*. 23 Feb. 2018.

SOURCE NOTES CONTINUED

Chapter 5. The Sangha

1. Joanna Cook. *Meditation in Modern Buddhism: Renunciation and Change in Thai Monastic Life*. Cambridge, NY: Cambridge UP, 2010. Print. 4–6.

2. Cook, *Meditation in Modern Buddhism*, 90.

3. Donald S. Lopez. *The Story of Buddhism: A Concise Guide to Its History and Teaching*. San Francisco: Harper, 2001. Print. 36.

4. Barbara O'Brien. "The Lotus Sutra: An Overview." *ThoughtCo*. ThoughtCo, 11 July 2017. Web. 23 Feb. 2017.

5. Lopez, *The Story of Buddhism*, 164.

6. Jeff Gordinier. "Jeong Kwan, the Philosopher Chef." *New York Times*. New York Times, 16 Oct. 2015. Web. 23 Feb. 2018.

7. David Gelb, creator. *Chef's Table*. Season 3, Episode 1. Netflix Original, 2017.

Chapter 6. The Sangha and the Community

None.

Chapter 7. Buddhism and the West

1. Denise Patry Leidy. *The Art of Buddhism: An Introduction to Its History and Meaning*. Boston: Shambhala, 2009. Print. 57.

2. "The Lengths to Which Some Will Go: The Self-Immolation of Thích Quảng Đức in 1963: Lesson Plan." *PBS LearningMedia New York*. PBS & WGBH Educational Foundation, 2018. Web. 23 Feb. 2018.

Chapter 8. Challenges

1. "Buddhist Extremist Cell Vows to Unleash Tranquility on West." *Onion*. Onion, 20 Nov. 2013. Web. 23 Feb. 2018.

2. "Over 600,000 Rohingya Have Fled to Bangladesh, UN Says." *Guardian*. Guardian, 22 Oct. 2017. Web. 23 Feb. 2018.

3. Hannah Beech. "Across Myanmar, Denial of Ethnic Cleansing and Loathing of Rohingya." *New York Times*. New York Times, 24 Oct. 2017. Web. 23 Feb. 2018.

4. Donald S. Lopez. *The Story of Buddhism: A Concise Guide to Its History and Teaching*. San Francisco: Harper, 2001. Print. 83.

5. Sam Harris. "How to Meditate." *Sam Harris*. Sam Harris, 10 May 2011. Web. 23 Feb. 2018.

Chapter 9. Buddhism Worldwide

1. Karen Larkins. "The Tranquil Zen Garden of Kyoto." *Smithsonian*. Smithsonian, Jan. 2008. Web. 23 Feb. 2018.

2. John Malkin. "In Engaged Buddhism, Peace Begins with You." *Lion's Roar*. Lion's Roar, 1 July 2003. Web. 23 Feb. 2018.

INDEX

ABOUT THE AUTHOR

A. W. Buckey is a writer and tutor living in Brooklyn, New York.